For Prosper, Roxane,
Guillaume & Natalie –
with big kisses – S.P-H. xx

For my very own bird
of paradise SNK – F.W.

First published in Great Britain in 2021 by Wren & Rook

HB ISBN: 978 1 5263 6270 4
PB ISBN: 978 1 5263 6272 8
E-book ISBN: 978 1 5263 6271 1
10 9 8 7 6 5 4 3 2 1

FSC
MIX
Paper from
responsible sources
www.fsc.org   FSC® C104740

Wren & Rook
An imprint of
Hachette Children's Group
Part of Hodder & Stoughton
Carmelite House
50 Victoria Embankment
London EC4Y 0DZ

An Hachette UK Company
www.hachette.co.uk
www.hachettechildrens.co.uk

Publishing Director: Debbie Foy
Editor: Phoebe Jascourt
Art Director: Laura Hambleton
Designer: Anthony Hannant (Little Red Ant)

Printed in China

Written by

Smriti Prasadam-Halls

Illustrated by

Florence Weiser

Dancing Birds
AND
Singing Apes

wren
&rook

In deep blue oceans, lush green forests, dusky dry deserts and even out in the furthest reaches of Antarctica, animals all across the world are saying **'I love you'** in their own special way.

Cooo!

Coooooo!

Croak!

Whether they are giving gifts, building homes, singing, dancing or showing off their beauty, courting creatures have many incredible ways of finding the perfect partner ...

The forests of tropical New Guinea hum and buzz in the glow of a sun-drenched morning. A **bird of paradise** takes centre stage.

...tap, tap, tap

Opening his feathers into a fan of deep and velvety black, he reveals a frill of shimmering electric blue, as bold and bright as his eyes. Turning and twirling, he hopes his dancing will impress his female admirer.

Nearby, a **bowerbird** is crafting a beautiful structure, with fruits and flowers. Carefully gathering colourful curiosities, such as buttons and glass, he decorates with flashes of scarlet and blue, green and gold.

Will this grand palace be enough to catch the eye of the finest mate?

Chirp, chirp

Deep down on the ocean floor,
a **pufferfish** tunnels through gleaming
grains of sand. He is making an
underwater castle.

Swish, flip, swish, flip...

He glides in and out, back and forth, flapping his tiny fins
to make the perfect pattern of peaks and valleys.

Glide, flap, glide, flap...

As a finishing touch, he adds shells and pieces
of coral to his delicate, circular sculpture.

Swish!

Flap!

At last, his sandy spiral is complete. He admires the spectacular nest and waits patiently for his sweetheart to inspect his work.

In the warm, tropical forests of Madagascar, a pair of **lemurs** leap from tree to tree. In furry suits of maroon and cream, they rub a sticky, smelly goo against the branches as they bound. They sniff each other's scent to get to know the other better.

Over time, their two scents mix to become one single perfume.

LOVE is in the air ...

Higher up in the trees, a pair of adoring **grey-headed lovebirds** sit beak to beak. In a flutter of feathers, one flits after the other. They preen each other's mint green plumes and feed one another morsels of food. These lovebirds will stick together for life.

The air is crisp and the sky is bright, as a determined male **gentoo penguin** searches for treasure among the rocks of the Antarctic.

Coo!

Caw, caw!

He seeks a stone so smooth and round that it will impress the perfect partner.

He has found the one!

He stands tall, puffs out his chest, lifts his head to the sky and gives a loud, trumpeting call as he presents his token of love. The female penguin accepts the pebble and they gracefully bow to each other.

Caw!

Together they will build a nest of pebbly gems in which to raise their little ones.

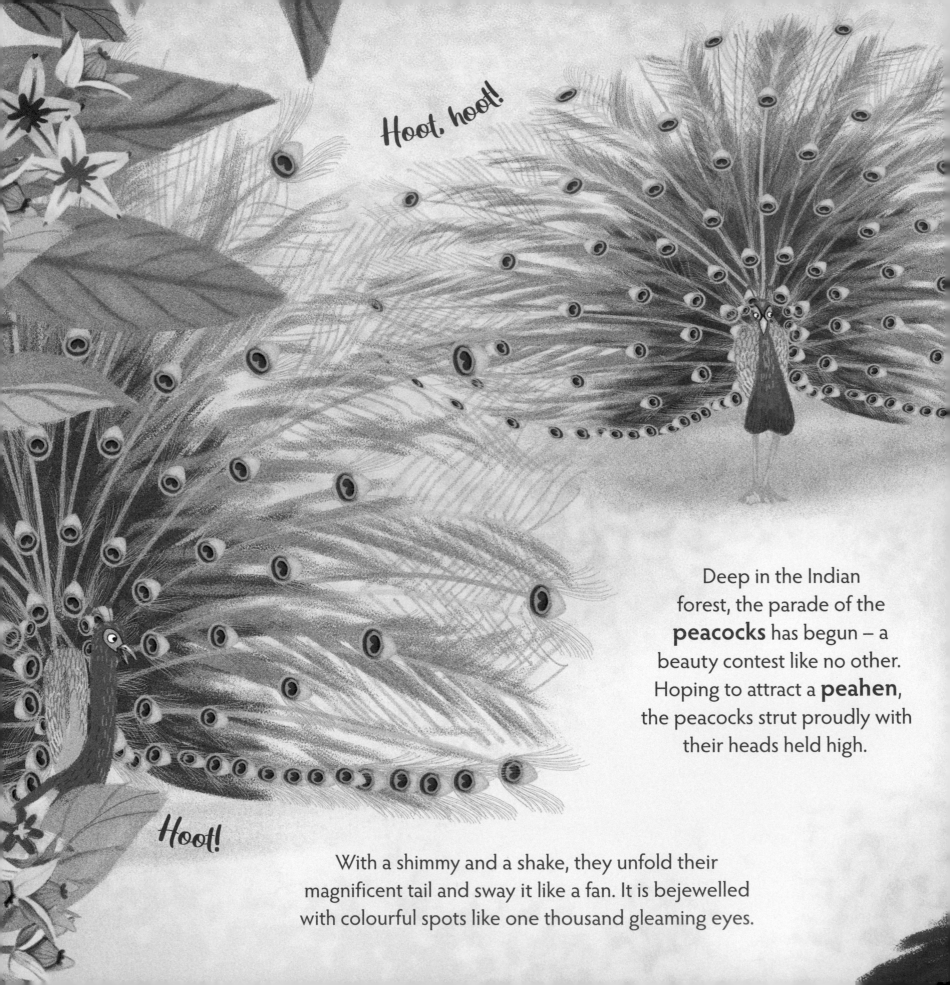

Hoot, hoot!

Hoot!

Deep in the Indian forest, the parade of the **peacocks** has begun – a beauty contest like no other. Hoping to attract a **peahen**, the peacocks strut proudly with their heads held high.

With a shimmy and a shake, they unfold their magnificent tail and sway it like a fan. It is bejewelled with colourful spots like one thousand gleaming eyes.

The peahen inspects the dizzying, dazzling
flashes of blue and green.

Who will be picked in this
flamboyant parade?

The Mojave Desert in California bursts into bloom. The dry, dusty earth blossoms with purple and yellow flowers. Then the **butterflies** come out to play. Sending messages through scent, their wings whir as they twirl a graceful, delicate dance.

In a small cluster, **painted lady butterflies** float in circles around each other. They spin and spiral, flit and float, searching for a sweetheart.

Flit, Float...

Meanwhile, a female **desert black swallowtail** perches patiently. Hovering males fly close by, but she will only choose one to flutter away with.

All around the desert, more and more beautiful butterflies dance on until they meet their mate.

Up in the treetops of Borneo's rainforest,
among the glossy green leaves, a male
Müeller's gibbon is on the lookout for love.
He calls out with a high, sweet song.

A female gibbon hears his charming
tune. She flies through the forest
towards him like an acrobat,
swinging from branch to branch with
her long arms and strong hands.

La, la, la! Whoooooop! La, la!

As dawn breaks, they perform a dazzling duet, which soars to the skies in harmony and resounds throughout the forest.

Soon, their young will join in with their tuneful song.

With a hop and a leap, a female **brown hare** skips across a spring meadow. A male hare bounds after her, a blur of fluffy fur. They race through the grass.

But this fierce female isn't impressed – and **she's** in charge! She stops the chase and they stand on their hind legs, paw to paw, face to face … it's time for a boxing match!

Then she scampers away to find a new partner.

Pow!

Beneath the hares' feet, sliding through the grass, a pair of **snails** inch towards each other.

They circle one another slowly before touching tentacles. As they move closer, a little love dart is fired from one to the other. With this small sign, the snails have chosen each other as a mate.

As night draws in on the Blue Mountains of Australia, a deep, grumbly growl is rumbling through the trees. It is the courtship call of a male **koala**.

Rumble, grumble...

Female koalas who are looking for love listen carefully to the sound and length of the deep bellow. They follow the sound to find their sweetheart.

Can you see me?

Meanwhile, the dusky
night lights up with the blinks
and winks of flickering **fireflies**.
The males' neon green flashes are
their way of asking, **'Can you see me?'**.
Watchful females wait in the leaves. When
they see a flash they like, they blink back
to say, **'Yes! I'm over here!'**.
Their twinkling language of light
sparkles in the dark, like
emerald stars.

Yes! I'm over here!

Honk, honk!

The waters are still. There's not a creature in sight and the Kenyan lake is silent except for the gentle murmur of the breeze …
… And then they start to descend. A flurry of pink feathers.

The flamingos have arrived!

Squawk!

Male and female, they move all at once. One million pink dancers step together, kicking their long legs in a spectacular show.

Turning their heads from side to side, marching together with beaks held high, they throw open their wings to show off their pink and black feathers. The flamingos are looking out for a dancer with a style to match their own.

Squawk!

Who will find love on this shimmering blue dance floor?

Vogelkop superb birds of paradise

There are more than 36 species of bird of paradise, and they can all be found in New Guinea. They are brightly coloured and have flamboyant courtship rituals. During the Vogelkop's dance, the male appears to change shape entirely when he fans his feathers.

Grey-headed lovebirds

The grey-headed lovebird is one of the smallest of the nine species of lovebird. They are native to Madagascar and the only species not to originate in mainland Africa. They are known for staying in the same pairs for life. They show affection by feeding each other from beak to beak.

Coquerel's sifaka lemurs

The coquerel's sifaka lemur can only be found in the rainforests of Northwest Madagascar. As they get to know their partner, they mirror the other's scent-marking behaviour of smearing and sniffing. When a pair produce offspring, they begin to smell even more alike than before.

Garden snails

Snails have a long, slow courtship that can last for several hours, beginning with cautious circling and a tentative touch of the tentacles. When they're ready, one stabs the other with a spike known as a love dart. Males and females perform similar roles during the courtship process.

Flame bowerbirds

The male flame bowerbird has brilliant plumage of orange and yellow. The female is olive green and gold. Their astonishing homes can be up to one metre high. In addition to flowers, their decorations sometimes include small found objects, such as buttons and glass.

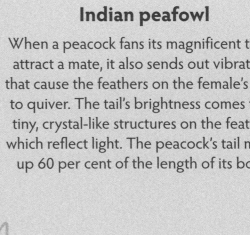

Indian peafowl

When a peacock fans its magnificent tail to attract a mate, it also sends out vibrations that cause the feathers on the female's head to quiver. The tail's brightness comes from tiny, crystal-like structures on the feathers which reflect light. The peacock's tail makes up 60 per cent of the length of its body.

Gentoo penguins

Gentoo penguins are the third largest penguin species. They form long-lasting partnerships and share the responsibilities for building their nest. When the female has laid eggs, both take turns to look after them; while one goes to feed, the other stays to keep the eggs warm.

Butterflies

California's Mojave Desert attracts many butterflies. Painted ladies have been seen circling each other in small clusters of two to eight for a quick 'dance', which scientists think might be part of their courting ritual. Among swallowtails, the males will go out searching for sitting females. Their courtship tends to last for about 45 seconds.

White-spotted pufferfish

The white-spotted pufferfish's extraordinary nests are constructed to attract a female. When she arrives, the male stirs up the sand in the inner circle in a final effort to attract her attention. The ridges and mounds are carefully created to hold the eggs, which will be laid at its centre.

Koalas

The male koala's growl is loud and deep and they use it to attract a mate. Females also make bellowing calls, but it is not known whether this is part of the courtship. Scientists believe that females can decode information about the male from his growl – the bigger the bellow, the bigger the koala will be.

Brown hares

Brown hares are known for their 'boxing matches' where they stand on their hind legs and scratch and hit each other. It is believed that they fight when the female doesn't want to mate with the male and wants to find a new partner. However, some say she may be testing his strength.

Müeller's gibbons

Gibbons use their singsong vocalisation for communication and courtship. They sing solos and duets in high, melodic tones. Once a gibbon finds a partner, they remain together and live in a family group with their young. You can spot a female gibbon's call from the accelerating whoops followed by a rapid series of bubbly notes.

Blue Mountains fireflies

Fireflies live most of their life as larvae below ground. Blue Mountains fireflies live above ground for a few days, during which they seek a mate. Their distinctive green flashing is very specific in sequence and males search for a female who will signal back with the same pattern.

Lesser flamingos

Over one million lesser flamingos flock to the Kenyan lakes each year to find a mate. Some scientists think that flamingos seek a partner whose moves in the courtship display closely mirror their own. Others say the brightness of their plumage could be more likely to attract a mate instead.

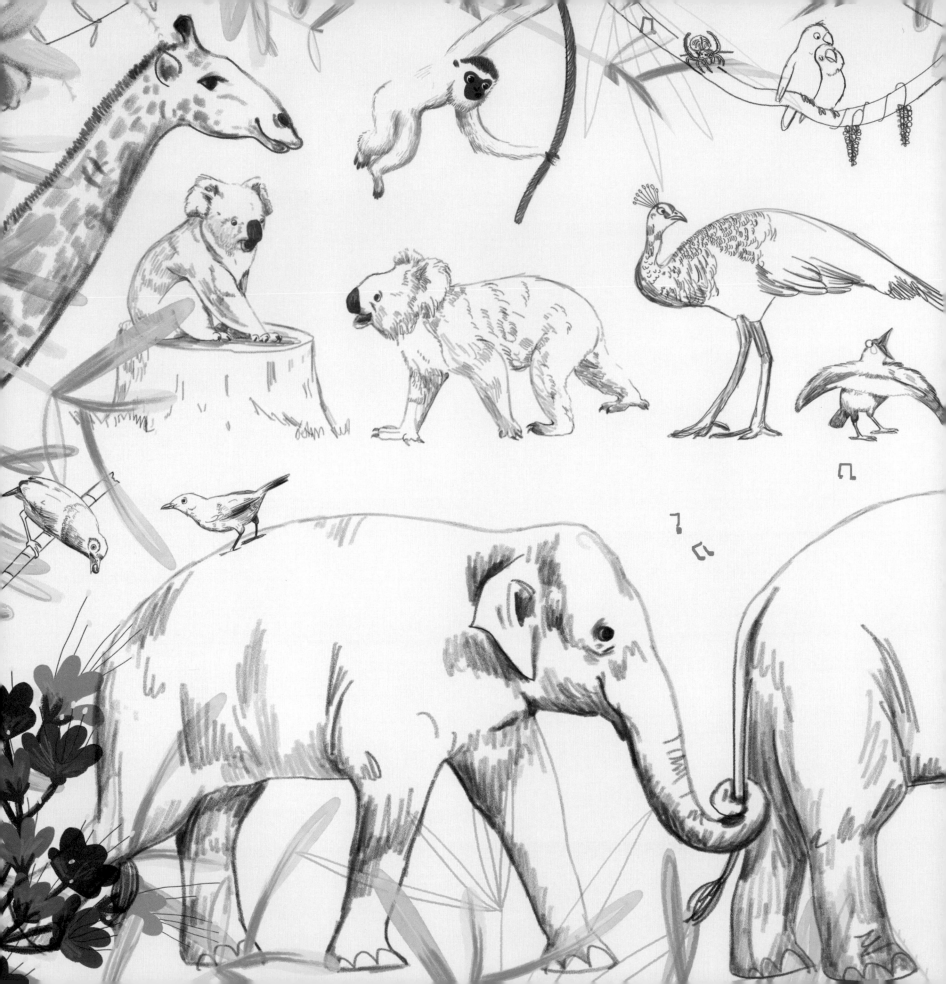